Look it up in Your ...

Oxford Advanced Learner's Dictionary

D1664637

Dr. Heinz Antor
Jacqueline Ward

Cornelsen
& OXFORD

Look it up in your ...
Oxford Advanced Learner's Dictionary 5th Edition wurde geplant und entwickelt von der Verlagsredaktion der Cornelsen & Oxford University Press GmbH, Berlin.

Autoren: Dr. Heinz Antor
                      Jacqueline Ward

Redaktion: Helga Holtkamp

Layout/Herstellung: Sabine Trittin

Illustrationen: Christine Georg

Umschlag: Volker Noth

Bestellnummer 112268

ein Arbeitsbuch zu   Oxford Advanced Learner's Dictionary 5th Edition
                     kartoniert, Bestellnr. 112250
                     gebunden, Bestellnr. 112233

1. Auflage
    5.   4.   3.   2.   1.   Die letzten Ziffern bezeichnen Zahl
 2000 1999 1998 1997 1996   und Jahr des Druckes.

Alle Drucke dieser Auflage können, weil untereinander unverändert, im Unterricht nebeneinander benutzt werden.

© 1996 Cornelsen & Oxford University Press GmbH, Berlin

ISBN 3 464 11226 8

Druck &
Weiterverarbeitung: Parzeller, Fulda

Vertrieb: Cornelsen Verlag, Berlin

Gedruckt auf Recyclingpapier. Hergestellt aus 100% Altpapier.

Contents

To the student

The aims of this workbook are to make you an efficient user of your new *Oxford Advanced Learner's Dictionary (5th Edition)* and to enable you to improve your English. As you work through the following pages, you will realize that your *OALD 5* is much more than simply an alphabetical list of English words and their meanings. Your dictionary also contains information on how to pronounce words and where to put the stress; if you are not sure about irregular verb forms, comparatives or plurals, you can look up these things in *OALD 5*; there you can also find the correct particles or prepositions that go with English verbs, information about the stylistic value of a word, collocations, idioms, phrasal verbs, differences between British, American and other varieties of English and much more. If you make the best use of the wealth of information offered by your dictionary you will also be able to produce better and more idiomatic English than before. We hope that this booklet will help you to do so and that you will have some fun doing the exercises. Working with *OALD 5* can be very interesting and enjoyable.

You may think that it is much easier to look up English words in a bilingual English/German dictionary. This may be true if you want to know the German word for *daffodil* ('Osterglocke, Narzisse'), say, and leave it at that. But if you look up the word *daffodil* in your *OALD 5*, you learn much more. You will then discover that some plants such as *daffodils* and *tulips* have *bulbs*, but that there are *light bulbs* as well and that the latter have a tiny *filament* inside that makes them glow. If you follow the cross-reference to the picture at the entry for *flower*, you will not only learn the English names of many other flowers and see pictures of them, but you will also know what the various parts of these plants are called. In other words, looking up words in your monolingual learner's dictionary rather than in a bilingual one will enable you to actively enlarge your vocabulary. Moreover, you will learn much more about the way English words are *used*, for example about verb patterns or about whether a word is used in formal or informal situations, etc.

One thing you should never forget when you do our exercises and when you work with texts later on is that you should *always* look up the words in your *OALD 5*, even if you think you already know the correct answer because you have come across the word before. You will be surprised how often will find that you would have made a mistake if you had not consulted your dictionary, and how often you will learn something new about the word even if you did know it already.

In the following exercises you will find examples of the problems that are particularly confusing and difficult for German learners of English. We have designed the workbook to help you avoid the mistakes often made in such instances. By working through this booklet, then, you will not only become familiar with all the different aspects of your *OALD 5*, but you will also profit from looking up words which have proved to be notoriously difficult for German students. We hope that you will become so attached to your dictionary that you will use it not only when you read an English text, but also when you have to write something in English yourself.

If you do the exercises in the order you find them in the workbook, you will see that we start off with relatively easy ones, and the exercises become more difficult as you work your way through the booklet. You can also do the exercises in any order, picking out the ones on aspects you think you particularly need to work on. Some of you may want to work in class or in groups, others will prefer to do the exercises on their own. You can check your answers by consulting the key *after* you have looked up the relevant words in your dictionary.

We hope you will enjoy working with your new *OALD 5*.

Heinz Antor and Jacqueline Ward

Looking up words with several meanings

Words you look up in the dictionary may often have many more meanings than you expect. It is important, therefore, to read through <u>all</u> the meanings given in the dictionary entry, before deciding which one is the best in the particular text you have to deal with.

A In the following exercise, you may think that you know the words in *italic* type, but they may have meanings you have not come across yet. Look up these words in your *OALD 5* and write down which of the definitions given is the correct one.

1 There were hundreds of *entries* for the New York Marathon this year.
2 My warnings *went* completely unheeded so that I am not surprised at the mess they find themselves in now.
3 He had *grown* to like her so much that he finally asked her to marry him.
4 Does this skirt *come* in all sizes?
5 When I sat down for lunch, my brand-new chair suddenly *gave* under my weight and I found myself on the floor. I really must go on a diet.
6 He hasn't left his *study* for eight hours. I really don't think this can be good for his health.

Words you look up in your dictionary ... bla, bla

cutting the lecture

7 I have only got fifty-*odd* pounds, which I'm afraid won't take us very far.
8 I still haven't finished my essay, but I got a week's *grace* from my tutor, who is very lenient.
9 I *cut* the lecture on how to use a dictionary because it was so boring.
10 She was *all* flustered about it.

B The word *hand* turns up in each of the following sentences. Complete the sentences with the appropriate words from the list below and explain the respective meaning of *hand* in each case.

> steal • tower • combine harvester • knelt • robbery • bad • pockets • broomstick • give • called • poor • clock • letter • nose • slept • collapse • asked • meet • laying • handle • small • suspected • whist

1 Take your hands out of your … when your grandmother is speaking to you.
2 It was almost midnight and the hands of the … were about to …
3 He … in front of her and … for her hand.
4 Can you … me a hand with … the table?
5 He is … of having had a hand in the …
6 If you keep giving me such a … hand, I won't play… with you any more.
7 The … was in such a … hand that it was almost illegible.
8 The farm-hand took me for a ride on the …

C Which of the following have got legs? Give a short definition of the meaning of *leg* in each possible case.

> wombats • tables • trees • cricket fields • football championships • aeroplanes • books • cars • round-the-world trips • roast turkeys • trout • trousers • legacies

Derivatives

A Look up these adjectives and make sure you understand them, then find the nouns derived from them.

1 bland
2 drowsy
3 plausible
4 pompous
5 queasy
6 self-confident
7 self-conscious
8 taciturn
9 repugnant
10 solvent
11 insane
12 jealous

B Now fill in the gaps in these sentences with a suitable noun from the ones you have found.

1 Despite the … caused by the rolling of the ship, we managed to eat several packets of crisps and some sandwiches during the Channel crossing.
2 My father's … on the subject of my pocket money makes me think he is not going to increase it.
3 His … is amazing, considering how little training or experience he has.
4 She was acquitted of murder on the grounds of temporary …

5 All the people who tested the new soup complained about its …
6 His love for her was still strong and he was suffering the pangs of …
7 The baby's … for stewed carrots was obvious from the way she spat out every spoonful her mother gave her.
8 After driving for nearly six hours, she was overcome with … and had to stop for a rest.
9 The … of the minister's speech was ridiculed by the Opposition, who called on him to express himself in plain English.
10 If my father doesn't increase my pocket money soon, I'm going to have … problems. I've borrowed money from several friends recently.
11 He would have liked to ask a question at the meeting, but his … made it impossible for him to stand up and speak in front of so many people.
12 The Defence Counsel questioned the … of her story, as there was no evidence to support it.

Homonyms

Some words in English have exactly the same form; their spelling and their pronunciation are identical. Yet they may have widely differing meanings, and they may belong to different word classes. In *OALD 5*, homonyms are listed in separate entries marked by small numbers after the headword (e.g. **port**[1], **port**[2], and **port**[3]). Therefore, whenever you come across a word you think you know, in a context where it doesn't seem to make any sense, consult your dictionary to see if it has another meaning. It may be a homonym.

Can you explain the meaning of the words in *italics* in the following very strange sentences?

1   The *page* was given a *page* of names and was asked to *page* first Dr *Page* and then all the others.
2   We will *foil* his plan to use the old *foil* for cutting through the silver *foil*.
3   The hairdresser cut off the contested *lock* and *lock*ed it away.
4   The plane *bank*ed steeply to the right so that you could not only see the *bank* I *bank* with but also the *bank* of the river it is built on.
5   *Can* I open this *can*? I simply adore *can*ned food.
6   I didn't carve your initials in the *bark* of your tree. You're *bark*ing up the wrong tree.
7   My spirits *rose* when I saw the beautiful *rose*.
8   Our *main* problem here is the electricity supply, because we still aren't properly connected to the *mains*.
9   After his company had *fold*ed up he returned to the *fold* and moved in with his parents, where his comfort was ten*fold*.
10   The beautiful valleys *lie* before our eyes, and it would be a *lie* to say that this isn't a glorious sight.
11   We *bit* off a *bit* more than we can chew so now we have to get the *bit* between our teeth. The trouble is that we've only got an old 16-*bit* computer, and it'll be a *bit* of a problem to finish in time with such obsolete equipment.
12   I only wanted to give my nose a good *blow*, but he misinterpreted the gesture and gave me a severe *blow* on the head. However, I hope that the scandal will soon *blow* over.
13   The captain put the helm to *port* so that the ship entered the *port* and the crew had a bottle of *port* to celebrate their safe arrival.

Compounds

Read the notes on compounds on Study Page A1. Choose words from the right hand column to form compounds with words on the left. Check in the dictionary to see whether they are written as one word, as two separate words, or with a hyphen. Use each word once only. (There will be some words left over on the right.)

billy • catchment • Catherine • lady • witch • turning • field • youth • car • milk • wish • copy • corner • rolling • zebra • skipping • nest • tumble • tip

figure • park • egg • killer • lock • hunt • rope • area • stone • maker • point • wheel • goat • shop • bone • crossing • drier • cat • hostel • tooth • head • toe • day • eater

Pronunciation

Your *OALD 5* always gives you the pronunciation for each headword you look up. This can be a great help in avoiding mistakes. You should always look at the phonetic information in each entry, because sometimes English words are pronounced quite differently from the way you might expect. Frequently, the spelling is not a great help, on the contrary, it may even lead you astray. Read the information on pronunciation ('Phonetic symbols', pp. 1430-31) on the inside back cover of your *OALD 5*, then do the following exercises.

A How are the following words pronounced? With /ʌ/, /ʊ/ or /uː/?

bush • dudgeon • rude • butcher • justice • gush • Buddhism • bug • bullfight • bully • bulletproof • but • fumble • fuddy-duddy • dull • full • lumber

B In the following exercise you will find words with similar or identical spellings. Look at how they are pronounced and find out which of the words in each case is the odd one out.

1 Rounded – bounded – hounded – wounded – founded – pounded
2 Cow – wow – mow – how
3 Zeal – heal – weal – real – deal – meal – seal – veal
4 River – quiver – shiver – diver – giver – liver
5 Gauze – mauve – gaunt
6 Toll – moll – doll – loll
7 Weight – height – sleight
8 chunk – chutney – chute – chubby – chuffed
9 Stool – school – brood – roof – rook
10 Crumbly – humbly – dumbly

C Many words in English are spelt with *-ough* at the end, but are pronounced quite differently. Find out the pronunciation of the following examples with the help of your *OALD 5*.

though • plough • through • tough • cough • hiccough • enough • thorough • rough

D Some English words sound the same but are spelt differently and have quite different meanings. Look at the sentences below and decide, with the help of the dictionary, whether the words in *italic* type are spelt correctly in the context.

1 As we were walking in the woods, a *dough* suddenly darted across our path.
2 There's a *fur* tree in our garden that we decorate at Christmas.
3 My sister has a real *flare* for dressmaking.
4 The *bough* was weighed down with ripe fruit.
5 Could you pick some parsley and *time* for me to put in this omelette?
6 The children want to go to the *fare* and ride on the dodgems today.
7 I haven't got *thyme* for gardening, my wife does it.
8 I've been kneading this *doe* for twenty minutes, shall I put it to rise now?

kneading the doe

8

9 I think it's cruel to kill animals for their *fir.*

10 The woodwork master showed her how to smooth the edge of the box with a *plain.*

11 Daddy, please stop the car, I must have a *pea.*

12 The conductor made a deep *bow* to the audience before leaving the rostrum.

13 The survivors of the crash sent up *flairs* to show the rescue team where they were.

14 He *wrote* his name in the dust on the window-sill.

15 Nowadays there is often no conductor on the bus to collect the *fairs.*

16 The princess in the fairy story could feel the *pee* through twenty mattresses.

17 It must have been uncomfortable in Elizabethan times to wear a *ruff* round your neck.

18 I don't believe in learning by *rote.*

19 My job is very tiring, but you have to take the *rough* with the smooth.

20 My husband likes good *plane* cooking, not fancy French recipes.

E Many words in English have different pronunciations depending on their meaning and on whether they are used as a noun, as a verb or as an adjective. Find out about the various pronunciations of the words in *italic* type in the following sentences.

1 Just a *minute*, but I don't think you are allowed in here. May I see you ID, please? His latest book contains a *minute* analysis of all the subtle differences in the pronunciation of words that look exactly alike.

2 I will *bow* to rational argument, but never to blackmail or violence.
Robin Hood with his *bow* and arrows was my hero when I was a child.
I have received an invitation to a big reception at Buckingham Palace, and I intend to wear my dinner-jacket and *bow*-tie.
The sea was quite rough that night, but the *bow* of the ship ploughed the waves unswervingly.

3 I don't want to *abuse* your generosity, but can you lend me fifty pounds for the trip to London?
He was convicted for child *abuse* and now has to spend the next eight years in prison.

4 I don't approve of his behaviour, but I expect he will have to *sow* all his wild oats before he will see sense.
Farmer Pilkington's *sow* has had seven piglets, and they are all in good health.

5 The *rebels* shot down a military aircraft with the Minister of Defence on board and thus destroyed all hopes for further peace talks.
When Tom was eighteen he *rebelled* against his father and refused to go to university.

6 I furnished my apartment with *reject* furniture to save money.
He proposed to her, but she *rejected* him so violently that he was heartbroken.

7 She was an *invalid* after the accident.
Your ticket is *invalid* because it has not been signed.

F Even if you know which sounds to use when pronouncing an English word, there may be a problem with stress. Where is the primary or main stress, and where do you have the secondary stress in longer words or in compounds? Your *OALD 5* contains the necessary information. Read the paragraph on 'Stress' on the inside back cover and then find out where the primary stress is in the following words.

put-down • visiting-card • garden suburb • hotel • label • to hang out • a hang-out • put-up job • garden centre • microwave • microwave oven • midnight • mid-range • lapel • municipal • principle • arsenic

Irregular comparative and superlative forms

When you look up an adjective or an adverb in your *OALD 5*, it does not only give you the meaning of the word. It also provides information on difficult, or irregular, comparative or superlative forms that are often a problem for learners of English as a foreign language. They are given after the headword of the entry and can help you to avoid mistakes. When a word has more than one meaning you should look at all the categories because there might be further information about which forms to use.

Complete the following sentences by using the correct comparative or superlative form of the words in brackets.

1 This is the (easy) exercise I have come across so far.
2 I have even (little) money now than before I met this so-called financial adviser.
3 He is a much (able) student than his lazy friend.
4 The (big) his lies became, the (mad) they sounded.
5 I didn't feel well when I arrived, but I'm much (well) now.
6 Don't be afraid of the doctor, the (bad) that can happen is that he will give you a little jab.
7 She is the (nice) little girl I have ever seen.
8 I have run out of petrol. Can you tell me where I can find the (near) petrol station?
9 He answered (many) questions than I had expected.
10 She is the (old) of the three sisters, and she lives in the (old) part of the house.
11 Everbody said this was the (messy) divorce they had seen for a long time.
12 The (good) your hi-fi is, the (much) trouble there will be with your landlady.
13 Any (far) questions? – Yes, Mr Travelwise. Which of your hotels is (far) from the big tourist centres?
14 He is much (clever) than one would think at first sight.
15 This is the (silly) thing I have ever heard.
16 He appeared much (humble) after I had told him off for his impertinent behaviour.
17 She was dressed in the (late) fashion.
18 When does the (late) bus leave Victoria Bus Station?

Irregular verbs

A Read this description of a day's events, which is written in note form in the Present Tense.

Wake early, lovely weather, spring out of bed, throw open window, do breathing exercises, have a shower, put on new jeans and shirt, make coffee and toast, sit on patio and read paper. Postman rings doorbell, brings small parcel and letter. Parcel contains Rolex watch from aunt who thinks it's your birthday. Letter tells you of lottery win and encloses large cheque. Spend next half hour phoning friends, plan a big party. Mum lends you her car, drive to supermarket, buy champagne, luxury foods etc. for party. Take Mum out to lunch, book theatre tickets for her and Dad for the evening, arrange for cleaning lady to do overtime – to help with party preparations and clearing up afterwards. At 7 guests begin to arrive, champagne corks pop, everyone eats, drinks, sings, dances, gossips, till the early hours, some go home, some sleep on the floor, some party till breakfast time, all say it was the best party ever.

Now write a letter to your aunt, thanking her for the present and telling her all about your day. Begin:

> Dear Auntie Pat,
>
> Thank you very much for the super watch. Last Friday certainly was my lucky day, although it wasn't actually my birthday ....

B   Rewrite these sentences, giving the correct form – Past Simple or Past Participle – of the verbs in brackets. Check them in your dictionary!

1   A serious problem has (arise) since our last meeting.
2   This recipe calls for eight stiffly (beat) egg-whites. What shall I do with the yolks?
3   The kidnappers (bind) the boy's hands together behind his back.
4   The goalkeeper (leap) high into the air and (catch) the ball.
5   The waiter (bring) the menu and we each (choose) something different to eat.
6   He (tell) her of the blitz night in Iraq and how the flames had (light) the sky.
7   When she (hear) voices in the hall she (put) aside her pencil and hastly (read) over what she had (write).

8   I (creep) upstairs, hoping my parents hadn't (hear) me come in so late.
9   As the fire (spread) through the forest the animals (flee) for their lives.
10 When I (pay) the taxi driver (swear) at me because I only (tip) him 20 pence.
11 When the film was (develop), I (find) that I had not (focus) the camera properly and most of the pictures were blurred.
12 I (offer) to lend him my bike, but he (prefer) to walk.
13 The lawyer produced a witness who (prove) that the defendant could not have (commit) the crime.
14 After he had (speak), the three of us (stand) there, silent in the darkness and the snow.
15 On the night before the exam I (dream) I was going to be (shoot) by a firing squad.

Countable and uncountable nouns

Read the sections on countable and uncountable nouns on Study pages B1 and B2 then do the following exercises.

A Complete the sentences, giving a plural form of the noun in brackets where possible.

1 The various (advice) she gave me were very helpful.
2 Thank you for the report, but I still need two more (information).
3 The workers in this factory earn good (money).
4 Our new flat is so big that we need some more (furniture) to make it homely.
5 I am looking forward to the (improvement) you have promised to introduce in the company, because there is certainly scope for (improvement).
6 I love exotic (fruit), for example (mango), (pineapple) and (kiwi).
7 Meeting my future wife and winning the pools were two (luck) on the same day.
8 We had a lot of (fish) when we spent a week in Sweden.
9 I was surprised at the great variety of (fish) I saw when I went snorkelling in Australia.
10 I always travel light, but Peter and Jill can hardly carry all their different (luggage).
11 We had some delicious (spaghetti) for lunch, but I didn't like the salad.
12 I would never have believed that you would make such rapid (progress).
13 Hurricane Andrew caused immense (damage) and took an enormous toll of (life) when it hit Florida a couple of years ago.
14 He took his dishonest partners to court and won a small fortune in (damage).
15 He was finally convicted on the weight of the (evidence) and sent to prison.
16 We had all kinds of (weather) during our holiday.
17 They are both in good (health) despite the quantities of (meat) they eat every day.
18 Hazel and I clearly have very different (taste): there's no way I would have married him.

There's no way I would have married him!

B Which of the options offered in brackets are possible? Why?

1 I have (a/some) bread for you, but I'm afraid there's (no/little/few) cheese.
2 Would you like (a/some) tea or (a/some) lemonade?
3 He has (a/some) knowledge many people would be glad to share.
4 Do you have (a/any) homework to do today?
5 Is there (any/a) butter left?
6 Have (another/some) helping of spinach.
7 She told me (a/some) news that sounded very strange to me.
8 I need (a/some) space as a private retreat.
9 I am doing this exercise as (a/some/any/several) preparation for working with my new *OALD 5*.
10 He speaks (a/the/some) very good English.

Plural or singular verb

It may not always be clear to you whether an English noun is singular or plural. You may think that a particular noun needs a singular verb when in reality it needs a plural verb and vice versa. Some nouns even take both singular and plural verbs. Sometimes it can be misleading to take the German translation of the noun as a point of departure, since the English noun may behave differently from its German counterpart. Your *OALD 5* helps you avoid mistakes by giving you information about what form of the verb is needed with a noun. Look up Study pages B2 and B3 on 'Nouns + plural verbs', 'Nouns + singular verbs' and 'Nouns + singular or plural verbs', then do the following exercise.

Complete the following sentences with the help of the appropriate form of *be* or *have* and decide whether it has to be used in the singular or in the plural or whether both are possible.

1 The news … very promising today.
2 The White House … threatened to cancel the peace talks scheduled for next Friday.
3 The crew of the ship … just started a mutiny because of the captain's cruel behaviour.
4 Physics … not exactly what I would call my favourite subject.
5 The audience … in stitches because his jokes were so funny.
6 The government … planning a new tax on dictionaries because there is so much information to be found in them.
7 Billiards … an entertaining game for anyone with an interest in geometry.
8 The army … fighting for control of the airport, which is the key to winning the war.
9 Rickets … a common disease in the 19th century.
10 The farmer's cattle … won many prizes in the past few years.
11 The United States … considered by many to be the only remaining superpower on earth.
12 Draughts … a game for the strategically-minded.

Irregular plural forms in English

Your *OALD 5* provides you with information on irregular plural forms in the relevant noun entries. This can help you avoid many unnecessary mistakes. So whenever you are in doubt about a plural form, consult your dictionary. It's worth the effort. Read page 850 on the irregular forms of nouns in *OALD 5* and use the noun entries to do the following exercise.

Complete the following sentences by putting the words in brackets into the plural.

1 They did not yet have electronic pocket calculators in ancient China, but they did have (abacus).
2 There have been so many (crisis) in the former Communist countries in recent years that one could easily forget how much has been achieved.
3 In ordinary mathematical graphs we usually have two (axis), a horizontal one and a vertical one.
4 The United States and the Soviet Union blocked many UN decisions with their (veto) in the time of the Cold War.
5 She spends her weekends in (disco) and (pub).
6 When you look at the (larva) of some insects, it is hard to believe how beautiful they will become one day.
7 Reason, tolerance and sincerity are only some of the (basis) of democratic debate.
8 In Disneyland you can relive the story of Snow White and the seven (dwarf).
9 When he came back from his trip into the wilderness, he was covered in (louse).

10 The old Conservative politician made a speech about law and order in Parliament and said that (thief) should be punished with the full severity of the law.

11 I have just received the (proof) of my new book from the publishers, and I hope to see it in print before the end of the year.

12 Many steamers with thousands of innocent passengers on board were sunk by the enemy's (torpedo) during the war.

13 The anthropologist was particularly interested in the (belief) and rituals of the tribe.

14 The farmer owns two (ox), three (pig), and twelve (sheep).

15 (Eskimo) live in the Arctic regions of North America and East Siberia.

16 The college sent a letter to all its (alumnus) and asked for contributions to the funding of a new chair in lexicography.

17 The illness was probably caused by very aggressive (bacterium) that have been unknown to us until now.

18 Even though it is incredibly hot in Death Valley in the summer there are (cactus) flowering everywhere.

19 This book has two (index) so that you can look for both names and subjects more easily.

20 We visited several (kibbutz) when we travelled through Israel last year.

Adjectives and word order

Most adjectives in English can be used both before a noun and after a linking verb such as *be*. For example, you can say *red roses* or *The roses are red*. Both uses of the adjective *red* are correct. However, some adjectives can only be used *attributively*, i.e. before nouns, whereas others can only be used *predicatively*, i.e. after a linking verb. In addition, a few adjectives can be used immediately after the noun only. Read study page B3 on adjectives and look up the entries for **attributive** and **predicative**, then do the following exercise.

Some of the following sentences are grammatically wrong. Why?

1 I never said I would resign. This speculation is pure.

2 The carpenter's work was accurate. All the drawers were true and fitted well.

3 We have known each other from immemorial time.

4 The sheriff said: 'I prefer alive bandits to dead ones.'

5 This was a mere rumour. But I'm not sure whether his slip of the tongue also was mere.

6 The body politic as a whole must not be jeopardized by individual actions.

7 Having worked on a farm during the summer, the alone ranger now enjoyed his freedom.

8 The main problem was that the awake lion could not be inocculated.

9 After the teacher had scolded him severely, the ashamed boy apologized in front of the whole class.

10 I could see that the children were watching a video nasty because the door was ajar.

11 The destruction of the village in the air raid was entire.

12 We are not in the farmhouse proper yet. This is just an outbuilding.

13 The president elect is soon to take office.

14 The nonsense of what she said was so sheer I simply couldn't believe it.

15 When she saw the ghost my aghast sister screamed so hysterically that the phantom disappeared again.

16 The notary public said he would charge 15 per cent if we reached an agreement and signed a contract.

Abbreviations

Abbreviations are listed in the dictionary as head-words in normal alphabetical order. What do the abbreviations in these sentences mean?

1 Patrick Friar, aka The Monk, looked at his partners in crime. 'Stealing the crown jewels from the Tower might be OTT', he said 'but we could try taking the ravens.'

2 After ten years in the USN he went into politics, joined the GOP and became an MC.

3 The RSPCA invariably gets more donations than the NSPCC.

4 GCSE and A Level results will be posted to candidates. NB No information can be given on the telephone!

5 The PM and the Rt Hon Humphrey Briggs from the FCO greeted MEPs in the VIP lounge at the airport.

6 'My son's got a BA and an MA', said Mrs Rich. 'That's nothing', said Mrs Law, 'my daughter is a QC.'

7 She worked for a CAD company. They have their HQ in WC 2.

Labels

A Read the notes on labels inside the front cover. Look up the following words and decide which is the odd one out in each group, and say why.

1 in clink – in the nick – in jail – inside
2 formica – polystyrene – plasticine – hoover
3 backside – buttocks – bum – behind
4 svelte – willowy – slim – skinny
5 balderdash – tommyrot – drivel – bosh
6 miser – saver – skinflint – penny-pincher
7 windshield – trunk – fender – bonnet
8 loo – latrine – convenience – powder room
9 council – counsel – plaintiff – tort

B Would you be pleased if someone described you as any of the following?

1 hoity-toity
2 namby-pamby
3 a clever Dick
4 statuesque
5 birdbrained
6 masterly
7 straitlaced
8 grandiloquent
9 a stalwart
10 a polymath

British, American, and other varieties of English

A Your *OALD 5* uses special labels for British, American, Scottish etc. expressions. Look at the list of abbreviations and labels on the front inside cover and on the following page of your dictionary, then do the following exercise.

1 Bill from Wisconsin and James from Sussex agreed to meet on the second floor of the Empire State Building. They both came, and yet they didn't meet. What happened?
2 In America, you need a ticket for the subway, in Britain you don't. Explain why.
3 The American word for lift is …
4 American men often wear suspenders in public, whereas their British counterparts would not even dream of doing so. On the other hand, it is a great honour in Britain to be a knight of the Order of the Garter, whereas this may sound a little suspect to American ears. Can you explain this?
5 Chips in England are a hot dish – and in America?
6 When Sam from Kansas City asked where he could find the rest room in the Regent Palace Hotel at Piccadilly Circus, he was shown to the …
7 Joey, my penfriend from Cody, Wyoming has a strange theory. In his last letter he wrote: 'The Fall presumably took place in the fall since there must have been ripe apples on the trees.' Can you explain this?
8 In the States, I love driving on divided highways. Do you also have them in Great Britain? Yes, we do, but they are called … here.
9 In Britain you can be as drunk as a lord. But the Americans don't have aristocrats. Does that mean that they are always sober and never drink any alcohol?
10 My American friends don't go to the chemist's when their doctor has given them a prescription for some pills. They get their pills from the …

B Where do the speakers of the following sentences come from?

1 I was bitten by a bug when I went out to the farm, and now I have developed a fever.
2 Come on, step on the gas, or we'll be late.
3 I know you would like to drive on, but if we don't stop at the next petrol station, we might not arrive at our destination at all.
4 The old castle is owned by Duncan Ross. He is one of the wealthiest lairds in the area.
5 Last time I was on safari I would have liked to sleep outside on the veld, but our guide said it was too dangerous. So we went to a hotel after all.
6 If she hadn't knocked me up in time, I'd have missed my train.
7 It's amazing how many things you accumulate over the years. Last time we moved I thought we'd need a whole freight train.
8 A: Where did you find that little china figurine on the mantelpiece over there?
   B: Oh that. It was quite a bargain. I got it at the jumble sale last Sunday.
9 I shouldn't have drunk that last glass of port yesterday. I must admit I'm feeling a bit crook today.
10 Our railroad system is a great monument to what true pioneer spirit can achieve in this world.
11 They have more than ten thousand sheep at this station.
12 We'll have to make further cuts if this company is to make it into the next century. I'm sorry, guys, but that's the way the cookie crumbles.
13 You can't hang this picture with just two drawing-pins. It's much too heavy for that.
14 Can you see that kook over there walking right in the middle of the street? He must be crazy.
15 Your car looks quite different to mine.

C The following short text is written in British English. What would it look like if an American had written it? You will need to change the words in *italic* type.

I went to the *theatre* last night to see my daughter as Rosalind in the first night of our local Thespian Society's 'As You Like It'. It was Moira's first major role, and we were all very excited. We had even invited some of our *neighbours*. Moira said she hoped she would remember all her lines, otherwise she would simply have to ad lib. I dressed formally, but I soon *realised* that I would need *braces* because I had lost quite a bit of weight after my last diet. It took me fifteen minutes to find them, so I was late when I finally left. I got into the *car* but it wouldn't start, and for some reason or other, I could not open the *bonnet*, so I had to walk. At least I didn't have to drive thirty miles on the *motorway* like my son Peter, who lives in a small village and can't get anywhere on foot. Although it was late *autumn* it was still quite mild, and I thought I might still make it in time. I was in such a hurry, however, that I didn't see the beggar on the *pavement* and stumbled right over him. He woke up, saw me in my *dinner jacket*, and called me a dirty capitalist. I didn't want to start *quarrelling* with him and rushed on. I knew I didn't have any time left and now regretted that the play didn't have a *prologue* that would have given me a few more minutes. When I arrived I was quite out of breath. I took the *lift* to the *first* floor, bought a *programme*, and went in. Unfortunately, my seat was right in the *centre* of a long row so that I had to disturb at least two dozen people. I had hardly sat down when the curtain went up. It finally turned out to be a *marvellous* evening and a great success for Moira.

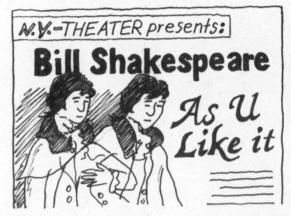

Prepositions

Your dictionary tells you which prepositions to use after an adjective. Look up these adjectives and find out which preposition they take, then choose the most suitable adjective for each of the following sentences. You will not need them all.

good • sorry • scared • full • accustomed • jealous • deaf • open • sensitive • greedy • happy • familiar • dependent • capable

1 The tyrant was … all pleas for mercy.
2 Jeremy was very … his baby brother.
3 Since Tom lost his job we've been … the state.
4 Although she is over 80, my grandma is still … new ideas.
5 Driving on the left seemed strange when we first got to England, but we soon grew … it.
6 I'm not … spiders, but I can't stand slugs.
7 My new sunglasses are … changes in the light.
8 She was an ambitious employee and … power.
9 Are you … walking home after all that beer, or shall I order a taxi?
10 My parents are not going to be very … my report this term.

Cross-references

You dictionary can only be as good as the use you make of it. This also means that your English will improve the more you use your *OALD 5*. That is why you should try and get as much as possible out of it, which means that you should not only read the relevant bit of an entry, say, the pronunciation of the headword or its meaning, but also try to profit from all the additional material you can find. Sometimes, you are there referred to another entry, an illustration, a 'Note on usage' or an appendix that contains further information relevant to the word you are looking up. These so-called *cross-references* are marked by little arrows (⇒), and you should follow the direction in which they point you. If you do this regularly, you will realize after some time that your English has become much more idiomatic and correct. The following exercise will show you how much you can learn by following up cross-references in your *OALD 5*.

1. The verb *snigger* means to laugh in a low unpleasant way. Find two more verbs that describe various similar ways of laughing, and give a sentence for each of them.
2. Sherlock Holmes always wore a *deerstalker*. What else could he have worn instead?
3. What's the difference between a *ton* and a *tonne*? In English, we distinguish between two different systems of measures. What are they called? A pound is a standard measure of weight. What other measures of weight are there?
4. Try to find an idiom with the word *time* and the name of an animal and then explain the meaning of the expression.
5. Find six verbs that describe the making of a request.
6. John's parents live in a *bungalow*. What other types of house are there?

7. Name the different parts of the leg.
8. The verb *prod* describes pushing something such as a finger or stick, into part of a person's body or into an object. Find four more verbs that would also fit this definition, describe the differences between them and give one sentence with each verb.
9. What has a *chrysalis* been before?
10. What kind of building is a *transept* usually found in? Name the other main parts of such a building.
11. A *haze* is a meterological phenomenon that consists of clouds of water vapour above the ground. Find three more terms for similar phenomena and explain the difference between them.
12. A *casserole* is a metal dish in which food can be cooked. Name six more such containers for cooking food in.

13 List five adjectives you can use to express that somebody is attractive and explain the difference between them. Give one example for each adjective.
14 Name at least three parts of a viola and find out what the equivalent to a piccolo's mouthpiece is called in an oboe.
15 Some people carry a *rucksack* when they travel, others have a … Find three words that could fill the gap.
16 How could one express that something happened not long ago? Explain the different usage of the words you find and give an example for each.

Usage notes

In some of the entries in your dictionary you will find a special note on how a word is used, or a cross-reference to a note at another entry. These can help you to choose the most appropriate word and use it correctly.

A Look up the word **possibility**, which is often used wrongly by German students, and study the examples. You will find a cross-reference to the usage note at **occasion**. Read the note and read the entries for the other words mentioned. Now decide which word fits best in the following sentences.

1 The end of the school term was a(n) … for great rejoicing.
2 If I had the …, I'd tell the Minister what I think of his education policy!
3 There is a faint … that I'll be offered a job in New York.
4 The … of winning the lottery are extremely remote.
5 He's usually very talkative, but on this … he hardly said a word.
6 There aren't many … for school-leavers without qualifications these days.
7 My father had the … to drive an early Rolls Royce yesterday.
8 This part of the coast is uninhabited, but it has great … as a tourist area.

B Now read the note at **shout** and the entries for all the words mentioned, then choose the best word for these sentences.

1 When the monster reared up and opened its huge jaws many people in the audience … in terror.
2 'You'll have to …, I'm a bit deaf.'
3 The crowd … angrily at the referee for sending the captain off.
4 As he was chopping the onion the knife slipped and he cut his thumb. He … out in pain.
5 The baby has been … nearly all night, she must be teething.
6 The children … with laughter when the clown's trousers fell down.

C Now read the entry and the note at **must**, and all the other entries referred to, then explain the difference, if any, between the sentences in the following sets.

1 a You mustn't eat the spinach.
  b You needn't eat the spinach.
  c You don't have to eat the spinach.
2 a I must get my hair cut.
  b I have to get my hair cut.
  c I'll have to get my hair cut.
3 a May I sit down?
  b Must I sit down?
  c Can I sit down?
4 a She must be tired.
  b She may be tired.
  c She might be tired.

Idioms

A Read the section on idioms on Study pages A6 and 7. The following sentences could all be made more lively by using an idiom in place of the words in *italic* type. For the first five you will find a suitable idiom under the entry for **leg**, for sentences 6-10 look for them under **nose**.

1 Our holiday in Bangkok *was terribly expensive*, but we had a marvellous time so it was worth it.
2 'You're not really going to get rid of the TV, are you Dad? *You were only joking*, weren't you?'
3 I'm sorry I'm late, but I met Mr Natterbox in the post office and I couldn't get away, *he never stops talking*.
4 My typewriter *doesn't work properly any more*, I think I'll have to buy a word-processor after all.
5 The headmaster must have given Gary a terrible talking-to, he came out of his room *looking very ashamed*.
6 *It doesn't make any difference to me* if the school trip to London is cancelled, I wasn't going anyway.
7 She has no right to *treat me like an inferior* just because she married a millionaire!
8 I get no privacy at home at all, my mum's always *interfering* in my arrangements.

9 If you just *keep going straight ahead* you'll come to the tube station in about five minutes. You can't miss it.
10 It really *irritates me* when he boasts about his exotic holidays, he knows the rest of us can't afford to fly to Bangkok!

B What idiomatic expressions of comparison could you use to describe the people or objects in the circumstances listed below? For example, if the sentence was: *A football player has scored five goals in a match*, you might immediately think of the adjective *proud*. If you couldn't think of it, you would look in the list of adjectives and find it there. You could then look up **proud** in the dictionary, and you would find the idiom **as proud as a peacock**. Choose from these adjectives.

stupid • miserable • bold • strong • drunk • dry • pretty • clever • inebriated • bright • tough • eccentric • sweet • nutty • proud • flat

1 Your baby sister has just been bathed and dressed up to go to a party.
2 A man staggers out of a pub singing loudly, and then falls over in the street.
3 A wrestler picks up his very fat opponent and throws him right out of the ring.
4 The opponent climbs straight back into the ring, apparently unhurt.
5 A child can read and write by the time she is three years old.
6 A man has just lost his job, his wife and his wallet.
7 A top hat has just been run over by a steamroller.
8 A girl takes back a blouse she stole from a shop and asks for a refund.
9 A plant hasn't been watered for weeks.
10 A lady keeps her food in the wardrobe and her clothes in the fridge.

Appendices

Your *OALD 5* does not only offer an alphabetically arranged list of entries from A to Z, but it also contains other parts that may help you to improve your English. You have already worked with the study pages, which explain some of the more tricky aspects of English to the learner and help you to use your dictionary more effectively. Now we will turn to the appendices at the end of *OALD 5*. These are sections that offer extra information, as you will see when you do the following exercises.

A   Answer the following questions with the help of appendices 1-5.

1   Which irregular verb does not have a past participle form?
2   List all those irregular verbs that have different forms in British and American English.
3   The past tense and the past participle form of the verb *abide* is *abided*. The alternative form, *abode*, is marked with an asterisk in the list of irregular verbs. What does this mean?
4   Some irregular verbs have more than one form for the past tense and the past participle. The verb *leap*, for example, can have both *leapt* and *leaped* as its irregular past tense and past participle forms. Similarly, for the slang verb *shit*, both *shitted* and *shat* are possible. Now find the one irregular verb that has three forms for both past tense and past participle. Give one example for each form.
5   Which is correct: *five hundred and sixty-seven* or *five hundred sixty-seven*?
6   'I called at half ten, but you weren't in.' Is this sentence always correct? What time does the speaker refer to?
7   Read the following short exchange and find out where the speakers come from:
DENTIST: 'If you only need a dental check-up, I could fit you in tomorrow at a quarter of ten. Would that be all right?'
PATIENT: 'I'm afraid I won't be able to make it before ten thirty.'
8   Where are the main and the secondary stresses when you pronounce the following number: two hundred and forty-nine ?

9   How do you refer to the following complex fraction in English: $68/375$?
10 Which of the following sentences is inappropriate? Why?
A: 'Can you come and see me at 10am?'
B: 'Sorry, that won't be possible because I never get up before eleven o'clock am.'
11 Where do you put the commas in the following conversation? 'I hope it's OK if I open the window' said the student in the first-class compartment. – 'Certainly not young man' the elderly lady replied 'because it would not be good for my asthma.' – The student retorted 'If you've got asthma, why do you smoke?'
12 Put the commas where necessary in the following two sentences.
My home town which is surrounded by beautiful mountains was snowed in last night. People who drink and drive should be sent to prison.

B   John has a big family. He tries to explain the relationships between all his relatives to his fiancée Mary. Complete his sentences.

Milly is my mother's sister and Jim's mother, so Jim and I are …. Dickie is married to my sister Libby so that he is my …. We call him Dickie, but Libby doesn't like that and keeps saying that his real name is …. However, when I point out to her that Libby is only short for … she says she prefers the more informal name. The only trouble is that she doesn't get on very well with Dickie's Dad. She never uses his name but always refers to him as her …. I would also like you to meet Gwendoline. She's Mum's grandmother, but whenever she talks to strangers or guests she proudly refers to herself as John's …. Libby is furious and keeps pointing out that she is her …, after all, and should also be mentioned by 'the old Victorian', as she calls her facetiously. Well, I'm afraid that with Libby you will get quite a pugnacious little … when you marry me.

Word-division

Word-division in English is not based on the same rules as in German. Therefore, it is always a point of some difficulty for the learner of English as a foreign language to decide where a word may be divided at the end of a line, and where not. Word processors sometimes can do the job for us, but only if we use an English-language system. The German version is of little help in this respect, and even English word processors sometimes make mistakes when it comes to word-division. That is why your *OALD 5* contains all the necessary information on this aspect of the language and tells you where words can be divided. Use your dictionary to check on the word-divisions in the following text.

Mr al-Rashid from Egypt was one of the dele-gates at the big international confer-ence that was held here last week. Whe-ther or not he really enjoyed the multifa-rious lectures and seminars will always re-main a riddle to the local organizers, be-cause the remarks he made just before the depart-ure of his flight back home were so myste-rious and vague that they could be interpre-ted in several contradictory ways. Be that as it may, the conference was a big success for the majo-rity of its participants, as the overwhel-mingly positive echo has shown. Neverthe-less, there are several things those respons-ible for the logistics of such a big ev-ent will have to bear in mind next time. Af-ter all, there is always scope for improve-ment, as Molly Prendergast, my late grandmo-ther always used to say.

Phrasal verbs

Read the section on Phrasal verbs on Study pages A2 and 3.

A Look at the examples of phrasal verbs under **make** and **get**, then complete the following sentences.

1 I don't believe it - you made that …
2 I can't make it …, he said he'd be in all evening, but there's no answer when I ring.
3 To make … for hurting his feelings, she bought him a CD.
4 When the sun came out at last, everyone made … the beach.
5 As I was walking along Oxford Street, a boy on roller skates snatched my handbag and made … with it.
6 This thundery weather gets me …
7 My mum is always getting … me to tidy my room.

8 It was such a shock finding that dead body in the woods, I've never got … it.
9 I hate getting … when it's still dark.
10 I ought to clean my bike, but I never seem to get … to it.

B Replace the words in *italic* type with a phrasal verb that means the same, using the verb in brackets.

1 She dropped lots of hints about what she wanted for her birthday, but her husband didn't *understand*, and gave her a scarf as usual. (catch)
2 We're having our kitchen *redecorated* so I can't cook a meal today. (do)
3 If the champagne runs out we can always *drink* white wine *instead*. (fall)

4 VC *is an abbreviation* for Victoria Cross. (stand)

5 He's rather a hermit, he *doesn't have much to do with the neighbours.* (keep)

6 I've been trying to do my homework for hours, but my brother keeps *distracting* me. (put)

7 'Could I speak to the manager, please?' 'One moment, I'll *connect* you *with* her secretary.' (put)

8 I'd just *fallen asleep* when the phone rang. (drop)

9 Let's go and see Pat, she never minds if people *visit unexpectedly.* (drop)

10 The film starts at 9.15 so I'll *collect you* at five to nine. (pick)

11 I don't like to *criticize* him all the time but he just doesn't work thoroughly enough. (pick)

Collocations

Read the section on collocations on Study pages A4 and 5.

A Explain the point of the following old joke.

B Now decide, with the help of your *OALD 5*, which of the words in brackets fits in the following sentences.

1 I try to eat as much (crude/raw/naked) food as possible.

2 'What lovely (stout/podgy/chubby) cheeks your baby's got!'

3 'What do you think of my painting? Give me your (candid/crass/blunt) opinion.'

4 Before we set off on the hike we were given (stern/strict/stark) instructions not to leave the footpath.

5 My boyfriend brought me a lovely (bundle/bunch/batch) of roses when I was in hospital.

6 To make a sponge you have to (beat/hit/strike) the eggs and sugar together, then gently (tuck/toss/fold) in the flour.

7 How many (faults/failures/mistakes) have you (made/done/written) so far?

Word patterns and structures

When you write a text in English, you will find that it can often be quite difficult to decide how the verbs you use combine with other words. Which prepositions can be used, is there an *-ing*-construction or an infinitive with or without *to*? All these are questions your *OALD 5* will answer for you. There are three different ways for you to find out about verb patterns in your dictionary:
- by looking at the examples,
- by looking at the patterns given in bold print in the entries (e.g. ~ **sb/sth (for/as sth** under **consider 1**), and
- by looking at the verb pattern codes in square brackets (e.g. [Vn], [V-adj], [V.*that*], [V.*ing*], [Vn.inf (no *to*)], etc.).

The following exercises will help you to understand how your *OALD 5* provides you with all the information you need on verb patterns.

A   Find out in which of the following sentences the verb is used correctly. Prove your answer by referring to the relevant examples in the entries for the verbs.

1   Could you please help me to carry this suitcase upstairs?
2   The missionary said that he needed more people to help him help the aborigines.
3   She asked the psychologist to help her father to help himself.
4   May I help you finding your keys?
5   You've been helping yourself to my floppy disks again, you impertinent child.
6   He said he would help me that I would have more spare time.
7   She said she considered him a rogue.
8   I replied that no one else considered him as a rogue.
9   She replied that she still considered him for a rogue.
10 I then said that I would consider her for the newly-created job of president of the office of slander.
11 She considered that this was none of my business.

12 She would not allow her sister to use her lipstick.
13 You must allow an hour for mowing the lawn.
14 Sorry, but I'm afraid we can't allow any conversation in the library.
15 She allowed that there might be something in what I said.
16 I cannot allow you talk to me like that.
17 He allowed himself another pint of lager.

B   Complete the following sentences by choosing the correct option from the words in brackets. Use the patterns in **bold** type given in each entry, to decide.

1   They tried to deflect her (against/from/ of/from) her chosen course of action, but all in vain.
2   I think that your new scheme will not commend itself (for/to/towards/against) the president.
3   After he had retired, he began to interest himself (for/on/in/with) gardening.
4   The dentist told me that I would have to cut (off in/low on/down on/back in) sweets if I wanted to keep my teeth.
5   She went (up to/through/towards/over to) Oxford after A levels to do a BA in English.
6   I substituted a new CD player (with/ against/for/to) my old record-player.
7   Don't waste your money (in/on/for/to) such an impossible business venture.
8   We had been racking our brains for hours, when suddenly this young apprentice came (in/on/up/along) with a brilliant new idea.
9   I would like to congratulate you (on/to/ for/with) your excellent school report.
10 She sallied (through/on/away/forth) onto the stage and insisted (in/on/to/for) thanking her audience in a long speech.

C   Read study pages B4-B8 on the verb pattern codes used in *OALD 5* before you do this exercise. You need not learn all the codes by heart, because most of them are self-explanatory. If you cannot remember what a particular code means you can look at the short explanations at the bottom of every page in your dictionary.

Find out which of the codes in brackets fit the following verbs. Give an example from the dictionary for each correct code.

EXAMPLE: explain ([Vnpr], [Vpr], [Vnn], [V.*wh*])
ANSWER: [Vnpr], e.g. *She explained her conduct to her boss* and [V.*wh*], e.g. *Can you explain how it works?*

1   decide ([V.*wh*], [Vnn], [Vadv], [Vn.inf (not *to*)])
2   prevent ([V.n *ing*], [Vn], [V.to inf], [V.speech])
3   raise ([V], [Vnpr], [Vn.inf (not *to*)], [V.*wh*])
4   start ([Vp], [V.*that*], [V.*ing*], [Vnn])
5   remember ([V.*wh*], [V.n *ing*], [V.speech], [Vpr])
6   invite ([Vn.*to* inf], [Vnp], [Vnpr], [V.*ing*])
7   limit ([Vnn], [Vnp], [V], [V-adj])
8   abide ([Vn], [V.*wh*], [Vpr], [V.*that*])
9   fail ([V.*to* inf], [V], [Vpr], [Vn])
10 mix ([Vnn], [Vnp], [V.*to* inf], [V.*ing*])

D   Which verb pattern code accurately describes the way the verb is used in the following sentences? Give at least one example for this pattern from the relevant entry.

EXAMPLE: I asked her a simple question.
ANSWER: [Vnn], as in *She asked them their names.*

1   Can you tell me why you did this?
2   Would you please refrain from smoking?
3   She looks very attractive today.
4   He insists that I accompany her to the reception.
5   I saw them exchange a secret glance.
6   'Nonsense!' Bill interrupted.
7   Shakespeare lived in England.
8   I saw her throw the dog out of the car.
9   I love eating and sleeping.
10 The general ordered the lieutenant to write a confidential letter for him.

Practice text: 'The Stowaway'

In the following text, a woodworm, which survived the
Flood as a stowaway on Noah's ark, gives its account
of the voyage. The report given here differs somewhat
from the Bible version.
Read the text straight through first, then try to do the
exercises that follow, using your dictionary.

There was strict discipline on the Ark: that's the first point to make. It wasn't
like those nursery versions in painted wood which you might have played
with as a child – all happy couples peering merrily over the rail from the
comfort of their well-scrubbed stalls. Don't imagine some Mediterranean
5   cruise on which we played languorous roulette and everyone dressed for
dinner; on the Ark only the penguins wore tailcoats. Remember: this was a
long and dangerous voyage – dangerous even though some of the rules
had been fixed in advance. Remember too that we had the whole of the
animal kingdom on board: would you have put the cheetahs within
10   springing distance of the antelope? A certain level of security was inevitable, and we accepted double-peg locks, stall inspections, a nightly curfew. But regrettably there were also punishments and isolation cells.
Someone at the very top became obsessed with information gathering;
and certain of the travellers agreed to act as stool pigeons. I'm sorry to
15   report that ratting to the authorities was at times widespread. It wasn't a
nature reserve, that Ark of ours; at times it was more like a prison ship.
Now, I realize that accounts differ. Your species has its much repeated
version, which still charms even sceptics; while the animals have a compendium of sentimental myths. But they're not going to rock the boat, are
20   they? Not when they've been treated as heroes, not when it's become a
matter of pride that each and every one of them can proudly trace its
family tree straight back to the Ark. They were chosen, they endured, they
survived: it's normal for them to gloss over the awkward episodes, to have
convenient lapses of memory. But I am not constrained in that way. I was
25   never chosen. In fact, like several other species, I was specifically not
chosen. I was a stowaway; I too survived; I escaped (getting off was no
easier than getting on); and I have flourished. I am a little set apart from the
rest of animal society, which still has its nostalgic reunions: there is even a
Sealegs Club for species which never once felt queasy. When I recall the
30   Voyage, I feel no sense of obligation; gratitude puts no smear of Vaseline
on the lens. My account you can trust.

(from A History of the World in 10¹/₂ Chapters by Julian Barnes, published by Jonathan Cape Ltd 1989,
© 1989 by Julian Barnes)

Now reread the text and answer the following questions with the help of your *OALD 5*.

1 The narrator describes the situation on board Noah's *ark* (l.1). What other *ark* is there, and what is it?

2 Which of the various meanings for *stall* given in the dictionary does the narrator used here (l.4)?

3 Which other word could the narrator have use instead of *tailcoats* (l.6)?

4 What would have been wrong with putting the *cheetahs* (l.9) within a short distance of the *antelope* (l.10)? How do you pronounce *antelope*?

5 Give another word or phrase for *inevitable* in the text (l.10/11).

6 The ark is like a small floating country. It has some of the characteristics of a military dictatorship. Which words in the text support this theory?

7 Find four examples of informal language in ll. 14-19.

8 When the narrator says he realizes that *accounts* differ (l.17), does he mean he has a banking problem? Which meaning of *account* is referred to here? Give the exact entry number.

9 What is the much repeated *version* mentioned by the narrator (l.17)? Give a synonym for *version* in this context.

10 What other word could one use for *charms* here (l.18)?

11 How do you pronounce *sceptic* (l.18)? Give a phonetic transcription. Is the spelling any help?

12 What is a *compendium* (l.18/19)? Give the plural form of the word.

13 Why is *myths* (l.19) a particularly appropriate word in this context?

14 When the narrator says that the animals are not going to *rock the boat* (l. 19), is he referring to the movement of the ark on the water?

15 We are told that the animals have been *treated as* heroes (l.20). What does this mean?

16 The verb *chosen* turns up several times in this text (ll. 22, 25, 26). What's the infinitive form of the verb? Why can the spelling be a

problem? What other words with a similar meaning are there? What are the differences between them?

17 In the text, the animals *gloss over* the awkward episodes (l.23). In the dictionary, the example given for *gloss over* is *gloss over the awkward facts.* Consequently, *gloss over* and *awkward* seem to go together very well. What's the linguistic term for this kind of phenomenon?

18 What's the opposite of *convenient* (l.24)? Why are the animals' lapses of memory *convenient*?

19 The narrator claims not to be *constrained* (l.24). Give another word that would fit here. What's the corresponding noun for *constrained*?

20 What is a *stowaway* (l.26)? How do you think this word came into existence?

21 Give a synonym for *flourish* (l.27).

22 The woodworm considers itself a little *set apart* (l.27) from the rest of animal society. What does this mean? Is the narrator proud of this or dispirited by it?

23 Which of the meanings given for *reunion* in the dictionary is used in the text (l.28)? Give the entry number and the definition.

24 Can you explain the name of the club some of the animals have founded (l.29)?

25 Why does the author use the word *Voyage* (l.30) when referring to his time on the ark? What other words are there to describe the activity of travelling? What are the differences between them?
Why does the narrator spell *Voyage* with a capital V?

26 The narrator mentions a possible *sense of obligation* (l.30) that may motivate the animals' behaviour. Where does such a feeling usually come from?

27 What are the prepositions you could use with *gratitude* (l.30)?

28 How do you pronounce smear and Vaseline (l.30)? Give the phonetic transcriptions.

29 Explain what the narrator says about gratitude putting no smear of Vaseline on his lens (ll.30/31).

30 Would you trust the narrator? Explain why or why not.

On September 13th a cavernous civic banquet hall in the north of England welcomed 76 European school students from 22 countries: finalists in the European Union Contest for Young Scientists. They had made their way to Newcastle after competitions in their own countries. The $300,000 bill for the event was paid by the EU, although some contestants came from outside the Union. It was a case (some will say a rare one) of EU money well spent.

Science fairs are less frequent in Europe than in America, where they help to foster scientific talent. The Newcastle fair shows Europe hardly short of that. Abstract mathematics, an ingenious retracting doorknob, a design for a human colony on Mars – the only common denominator among these Euro-projects was youth, enthusiasm and excellent spoken English.

Some of the work needed sophisticated equipment. One aspiring Danish evolutionary biologist used the local university laboratories to analyse DNA from crocodiles, chickens and pythons; a high-tech German trio studied the spread of viruses. But much of what was on show required little money or machinery. In a sequence of simple experiments, a Dutch team showed that children are better at remembering and reproducing colours if they know words for many different shades. Memory for colours depends, in part, on language.

A pair of Irish lads devised a way to hear thirsty plants. If a plant loses water to the air faster than it sucks it from the soil, tiny bubbles form in the tubes that carry sap from the roots to the leaves. When a bubble forms, it makes a noise – an event known as cavitation. By listening in with an amplifier, the boys learned to detect the sound of leaves starting to wilt. They envisage automatic watering systems that would turn on whenever the frequency of cavitations showed plants were thirsty.

Then there were the inventions. A writing machine whirred away, spelling out phrases in the creator's loopy hand (it is good enough to sign his cheques). The retracting doorknob already has a patent – and might be seen in Austrian public lavatories some time next year.

True, the contest is dwarfed by the British Association's Annual Festival of Science at the University of Newcastle across the street, but it is growing fast. Results from the previous six years suggest that the youngsters go on to study science at university. But in one respect, the young scientists bear a depressing similarity to their older counterparts over the road. Of the 76, only 12 are girls.

A Read the article straight through once, then read it again in detail and use your *OALD 5* to help you answer these questions.

1 In which sense is the word *civic* (l.1) used here? Why is the word MUNICIPAL printed in capital letters in the entry for *civic*? (If you don't know, look at the Key to dictionary entries on page vii)
2 What word should the writer really have used rather than *banquet* (l.1) to describe the hall?
3 *Finalists* (l.2) are contestants – but are all contestants finalists?
4 If a banqueting hall is a place where banquets are held, and a dance hall is a place for dancing, is a *music-hall* the place you would go to hear a concert?
5 What is the difference between a *final* and a *finale*?
6 What do the initials *EU* stand for?
7 Is the word *case* (l.6) used in its legal sense here?
8 Which definition of *fair* (l.8) is meant here? What other words can be used for such events?
9 Give a synonym for *foster* (l.9). What do we call people who for a limited period look after a child that is not their own?
10 Explain the phrase *hardly short of that* (l.9/10) in your own words. Which definitions of *hardly* and *short* are meant here? (Give the entry numbers.)
11 Does the writer think the *retracting doorknob* is a good invention? Which word tells you this?
12 What else can be retracted, in the other senses of the word?
13 In what area is the phrase *the common denominator* (l.11) normally used?
14 Apart from machinery or equipment, what else can be described as *sophisticated* (l.14)?
15 Why is the Danish biologist described as *aspiring* (l.14)?
16 How many people were there in the German team studying the spread of viruses?
17 *Shade* (l.20) has several different meanings. In which sense is it used here? (Give the entry number). What else can it mean in the plural?

18 *Soil* (l.23) is used here as a noun. What does it mean as a verb?
19 What word is used for the liquid that carries food to all parts of a plant? What does this word mean when it is applied to a person?
20 In what other contexts can the verb *wilt* (l.26) be used? Give an example!
21 What word would Americans use for *envisage* (l.27)?
22 Which of the following things *whirr* (l.29): a top; a cat; a sewing machine; a computer; a moth's wings?
23 Explain the meaning of *away* (l. 29) after *whirred*.
24 You will find the word *loopy* (l.30) in the dictionary. Is the definition given the right one in this context? If not, can you work out the meaning from another entry?
25 In what ways are the *British Association's Festival of Science* and the *European Union Contest for Young Scientists* (a) different (b) alike?

B Now fill in the gaps in these sentences with words from the text.

1 One of the … in the quiz show had been given the answers in advance.
2 I can't go to the concert with you, I'm very … of cash this month.
3 It's a matter of … pride to keep our historic Town Hall in good repair.
4 The aim of the twin-town scheme is to … good relations with our … in other countries.
5 Diana won't want to go to a cafeteria with you, she's got much more … tastes.
6 After three hours of sightseeing I was beginning to …, but our guide insisted on us visiting the National Gallery before lunch.
7 My sister has invented an … gadget for painting her toenails.
8 The … in our garden is very rich, so we grow all our own vegetables.
9 My mother has knitted me a pullover in a hideous … of purple.
10 There have been an unusual number of … of leukaemia in the area around Sellafield.

My mother died when I was born, which makes me sound princess-like and quaint. From the beginning people have said that I am old-fashioned. In Yorkshire to be old-fashioned means to be fashioned-old, not necessarily to be out-of-date, but I think I am probably both. For it is rather out-of-date,

5 even though I will be eighteen this February, to have had a mother who died when one was born and it is to be fashioned-old to have the misfortune to be and look like me.

    I emerged into this cold house in this cold school in this cold seaside town where you can scarcely even get the telly for the height of the hills

10 behind – I emerged into this great sea of boys and masters at my father's school (St Wilfrid's) an orange-haired, short-sighted, frog-bodied ancient, a square and solemn baby, a stolid, blinking, slithery-pupilled (it was before they got the glasses which straightened the left eye out) two-year-old, a glooming ten-year-old hanging about the school cloisters ('Hi Bilgie,

15 where's your broomstick?') and a strange, thickset, hopeless adolescent, friendless and given to taking long idle walks by the sea.

    My father – a Housemaster – is known to the boys as Bill. My name is Marigold, but to one and all because my father is very memorable and eccentric and had been around at the school for a very long time before I

20 was born – I was only Bill's Daughter. Hence Bilgewater. Oh hilarity, hilarity! Bilgewater Green.

    I will admit freely that I very much like the name Marigold. Marigold Daisy Green is my true and christened name and I think it is beautiful. Daisy was my mother's name and also comes into Chaucer.* Daisy, the day's eye, the

25 eye of day, as my dear Uncle Edmund Hastings-Benson now and then reminds me (he teaches English as well as Maths). It seems a great bitterness that anyone with a name as beautiful as Marigold Day's-eye Green should be landed with Bilgewater instead however appropriate this may be. 'In the end', says somebody, 'almost everything is appropriate', and indeed

30 over the years the boys have had a peculiar flair for hitting on the right word for a nickname.

Nick-name. Old Nick's name. Bilgewater.
Bilgewater Green.

(From 'Bilgewater' by Jane Gardam, published by Hamish Hamilton Children' s Books Ltd 1976,
© 1976 Jane Gardam)

* Geoffrey Chaucer (c.1343–1400), English poet, most famous for his 'Canterbury Tales.'

A Read the extract once straight through, without looking anything up, to get a general impression of the narrator, then see if you can answer these questions.

1 How old is she?
2 Where does she live?
3 What is her real name?
·4 What is her nickname?
5 Does she like her nickname?
6 How did she get her nickname?

B Now read it again, and look up all the unfamiliar words in your *OALD 5*. Some of them are unusual words or compounds which you will not find in the dictionary in exactly this form, so you will have to look up their separate parts or the words they are derived from. Then answer the following questions.

1 What is the difference between *old-fashioned* (l.2) and *fashioned-old*? (l.3) Which definition of old is meant in *fashioned-old*? (Give the entry number)
2 The writer uses the verb *emerge* twice. (l.8 and l.10). Does it have exactly the same meaning each time?
3 What does the word *for* mean in the phrase *for the height of the hills behind* (l.9/10) (Give the entry number).
4 Which two words tell us why Marigold had to wear glasses?
5 Explain *frog-bodied* (l.11) and give three other examples of compounds formed with *-bodied*.
6 Which definition of pupil did you need in order to understand *slithery-pupilled*? (l.12). What is the other meaning of *pupil*?
7 The word *blinking* (l.12) is listed in the dictionary. Is it used here in the sense given? If not, where can you find its meaning?
8 Which two words suggest that Marigold often didn't have anything particular to do?

9 Does *Housemaster* (l.17) mean the same thing as *the master of the house*?
10 What did the boys mean when they asked her where her *broomstick* (l.15) was?
11 Is there any clue in the passage as to why she was christened Marigold?
12 Why do you think she says her nickname may be appropriate?
13 Look at the guide to the pronunciation of *appropriate* (l.28). Is the verb *to appropriate* pronounced in the same way?

C Fill in the gaps in the sentences below with words chosen from the list, all of which were found in the passage. You will not need them all.

misfortune • shortsighted • quaint • solemn • cloisters • slithery • hilarity • idle • stolid • for • telly • appropriate

1 There was great … among the boys when the new teacher dropped the chalk he had been nervously throwing in the air.
2 You needn't look so …, this is a wedding, not a funeral!
3 We've got far too much information in this report, you can't see the wood … the trees.
4 It was hot and crowded in the town so we were glad to escape to the cool peace of the cathedral … where the monks used to walk.
5 The holiday cottage was very …, but the ceilings were very low and I got sick of bumping my head on the beams.
6 It had rained all night and the steep path to the beach was very …
7 Poppy came down to breakfast wearing a tight miniskirt and high-heeled shoes but her mother said this was not … dress for a sailing trip, so she had to change.
8 My mother can't bear to be …, even when she is watching television she has to knit at the same time.

Key

Looking up words with several meanings

A

1 entry 4 ~ (for sth) (a) [C] = a person or thing competing in a contest, race, etc.

2 go[1] State 14 = (used with a negative past participle to show that an action does not happen).

3 grow 5 = to reach the point or stage at which one does the specified thing

4 come 5 ~ in sth = to be available

5 give[1] Other meanings 20 = to bend or stretch under pressure

6 study[1] 5 = a room, esp in sb's home, used for reading and writing.

7 odd 4 = a little more than

8 grace 3 = extra time allowed to renew a licence, pay a bill, etc after the day when it is due.

9 cut[1] 9 = to stay away from a lesson, meeting, etc; to fail to attend sth.
or 6 = to reduce sth by removing a part of it.

10 all[5] 2 = very.

B

1 pockets (hand[1] 1).

2 clock, meet (hand[1] 4).

3 knelt, asked (hand[1] 10).

4 give, laying (hand[1] 2).

5 suspected, robbery (hand[1] 3).

6 bad, whist (hand[1] 8(a)).

7 letter, bad (hand[1] 9).

8 combine harvester (hand[1] 5 (a)).

C

wombats (leg 1), tables (leg 4), cricket fields (leg 6), football championships (leg 5(b)), round-the-world trips (leg 5(a)), roast turkeys (leg 2), trousers (leg 3).

Derivatives

1 blandness	7 self-consciousness
2 drowsiness	8 taciturnity
3 plausibility	9 repugnance
4 pomposity	10 solvency
5 queasiness	11 insanity
6 self-confidence	12 jealousy

Sentences:

1 queasiness	7 repugnance
2 taciturnity	8 drowsiness
3 self-confidence	9 pomposity
4 insanity	10 solvency
5 blandness	11 self-consciousness
6 jealousy	12 plausibility

Homonyms

The homonyms in this exercise are used in the following meanings:

1 page[3] (a); page[1] (b); page[2] 1; Page is a proper name.

2 foil[2]; foil[3]; foil[1] 1.

3 lock[3] 1; lock[2] phr v lock sth away.

4 bank[2]; bank[3] 1; bank[4] 1; bank[1] 1.

5 can[2] 2 (b); can[1] 2 (a); can[1] > can v.

6 bark[1]; bark[2] > bark v idm bark up the wrong tree.

7 rose[1] = rise[2] 8 (pt rose); rose[2].

8 main[1]; main[2].

9 fold[1] 3 (a); fold[2] 2; -fold.

10 lie[2] 4; lie[1] > lie n.

11 bit[4] = bite[1] idm bite off more than one can chew; bit[1] 1 (b); bit[2] idm get/take the bit between one's/the teeth; bit[3]; bit[1] 1 (b).

12 blow[2]; blow[3] 1; blow[1] phr v blow over.

13 port[2]; port[1] 2; port[3] (a).

Compounds

skipping-rope • turning-point • Catherine wheel • witch-hunt • catchment area • zebra crossing • car park • billy-goat• milk tooth • field-day • youth hostel • tiptoe • nest egg • wishbone • copycat • lady-killer • rolling stone • corner shop • tumble-drier

Pronunciation

A

The following words are pronounced with /ʌ/: *dudgeon, justice, gush, bug, but, fumble, fuddy-duddy, dull, lumber.* Words which are pronounced with an /ʊ/: *bush, butcher, Buddhism, bullfight, bully, bulletproof, full.* The only word in this list that is pronounced with an /uː/ is *rude.*

B

1 wounded (/uː/ instead of /aʊ/).

2 mow (/əʊ/ instead of /aʊ/).

3 real (/iːə/ instead of /iː/).

4 diver (/aɪ/ instead of /ɪ/).

5 mauve (/əʊ/ instead of /ɔː/).

6 toll (/əʊ/ instead of /ɑ/).

7 weight (/eɪ/ instead of /aɪ/).

8 chute (/ʃuː/ instead of /tʃʌ/).

9 rook (/ʊ/ instead of /uː/).

10 dumbly (/ml/ instead of /mbl/).

C

though /ðəʊ/; plough /plaʊ/; through /θruː/; tough /tʌf/; cough /kɑf/; hiccough /'hɪkʌp/; enough /ɪ'nʌf/; thorough /'θʌrə/; rough /rʌf/.

32

D

1 Wrong, *doe*
2 Wrong, *fir*
3 Wrong, *flair*
4 Right
5 Wrong *thyme*
6 Wrong, *fair*
7 Wrong, *time*
8 Wrong, *dough*
9 Wrong, *fur*
10 Wrong, *plane*

11 Wrong, *pee*
12 right
13 Wrong, *flares*
14 Right
15 Wrong, *fares*
16 Wrong, *pea*
17 Right
18 Right
19 Right
20 Wrong, *plain*

E

1 /'mɪnɪt/; /maɪ'njuːt/.
2 /baʊ/; /bəʊ/; /bəʊ/; /baʊ/.
3 /ə'bjuːz/; /ə'bjuːs/.
4 /səʊ/; /saʊ/.
5 /'reblz/; /rɪ'beld/.
6 /'riːdʒekt/; /rɪ'dʒektɪd/.
7 /'ɪnvəlɪd/; /ɪn'vælɪd/.

F

'put-down – 'visiting-card – ˌgarden 'suburb – /həʊ'tel/ – /'leɪbl/ – to ˌhang 'out – a 'hang-out – ˌput-up 'job – 'garden centre – 'microwave – ˌmicrowave 'oven – /'mɪdnaɪt/ – /ˌmɪd'reɪndʒ/ – /lə'pel/ – /mjuː'nɪsɪpl/ – /'prɪnsəpl/ – /'ɑːsnɪk/.

Irregular comparative and superlative forms

1 easiest
2 less, *note at* much
3 abler/more able
4 bigger, madder
5 better
6 worst
7 nicest
8 nearest
9 more

10 eldest, oldest
11 messiest
12 better, more
13 further, furthest/farthest
14 cleverer
15 silliest
16 humbler
17 latest
18 last

Irregular verbs

A *(possible solution)*

I woke up early and it was a lovely day, so I sprang out of bed and threw open the window and did some breathing exercises. Then I had a shower and put on my new jeans and shirt. I made some coffee and toast, sat on the patio and read the paper while I was eating my breakfast. Suddenly the doorbell rang. It was the postman, who brought me a small parcel and a letter. The parcel of course contained the watch from you, and the letter told me that I had won a lottery prize, and enclosed a cheque for £1000! I spent the next half an hour phoning all my friends, and we planned to have a big party that evening. Mum lent me her car and I drove to the supermarket and bought champagne, smoked salmon and strawberries and ice cream for the party. I took Mum out for lunch, and I booked theatre tickets for her and Dad for the evening. I also arranged for our cleaning lady to do some overtime, to help with the clearing up. The guests began to arrive at 7, the champagne corks were soon popping, and everyone ate and drank, sang, danced and gossiped till the early hours. Some people went home, some slept on the floor, but some partied until breakfast time. They all said it was the best party ever! And incidentally, everyone admired my Rolex!   With lots of love from …

B

1 arisen
2 beaten
3 bound
4 leapt/leaped, caught
5 brought, chose
6 told, lit/lighted
7 heard, put, read, written
8 crept, heard

9 spread, fled
10 paid, swore, tipped
11 developed, found, focused/focussed
12 offered, preferred
13 proved, committed
14 spoken, stood
15 dreamt/dreamed, shot

Countable and uncountable nouns

A

1 pieces/words of advice (advice is [U]).
2 bits/pieces of information (information is [U]).
3 money (no plural form in sense 3).
4 (pieces of) furniture (furniture is [U]).
5 improvements ([C] in sense 1b); improvement ([U] in sense 1a).
6 fruit(s) ([C, U]), mangoes, pineapples, kiwi.
7 strokes of luck (luck is [U]).
8 fish (cf. note at fish, the speaker of this sentence does not refer to different species of fish).
9 fishes (i.e. the speaker here refers to different species of fish rather than just the sheer number of fish).
10 pieces of luggage (luggage is [U]).
11 spaghetti (spaghetti is [U]).
12 progress (progress is [U]).
13 damage (damage is [U] in sense 1); life (life is [U] in sense 3)
14 damages (sense 2).
15 evidence (evidence is [U] in sense 1).
16 weather (weather is [U]).
17 health (health is [U]), meat(s) ([U, C]).
18 tastes([C, U] in sense 5).

B

1 some (bread is [U]), no/little (cheese is [U] in sense a).
2 some (tea is [U] in sense 1b)/a (if tea is used in sense 1c), some/a (lemonade is [U, C]).
3 some (knowledge is [U]).
4 any (homework is [U]).
5 any (butter is [U]).
6 another (helping is not marked [U] so that some would not make sense)
7 some (news is [U]).
8 some (space is [U] in sense 2).
9 a (preparation is [U] in sense 1a).
10 — (English is [U]).

Plural or singular verb

1 is	7 is
2 has/have	8 is/are
3 has/have	9 was
4 is	10 have
5 was/were	11 is/are
6 is/are	12 is

Irregular plural forms in English

1 abacuses	12 torpedoes
2 crises	13 beliefs
3 axes	14 oxen, pigs, sheep
4 vetoes	15 Eskimo/Eskimos
5 discos, pubs	16 alumni
6 larvae	17 bacteria
7 bases	18 cacti/cactuses
8 dwarfs/dwarves	19 indexes (sense 1a; the
9 lice	alternative form indices
10 thieves	is used in sense 2)
11 proofs	20 kibbutzim

Adjectives and word order

1 Wrong. *Pure* in sense 2 (nothing but, complete, sheer) is attributive. One could only say: This is pure speculation.
2 Correct. *Accurate* is unmarked in the dictionary and can therefore be used both attributively and predicatively. *True* is used predicatively here in sense 5 (fitted or placed in its proper, esp upright, position).
3 Wrong. *Immemorial* is one of the adjectives that can be used immediately after the noun only. It only turns up in the phrase *from/since time immemorial*.
4 Wrong. *Alive* is used predicatively only.
5 *Mere* can only be used attributively. Therefore, *a mere rumour* is correct, but *his slip of the tongue also was mere* is wrong.
6 Correct. Cf. the cross-reference to *body politic* at *politic*. *Individual* is attributive.
7 Wrong. *Alone* is used predicatively only.
8 Wrong. *Awake* is used predicatively only.
9 Wrong. *Ashamed* is used predicatively only.
10 Correct. *Ajar* is predicative. *Nasty* here is used as a noun (cf. the entry at *video nasty*).
11 Wrong. *Entire* is used attributively only.
12 Correct. *Proper* in sense 1b (in its true form, itself) is one of the adjectives that are used immediately after the noun.
13 Correct. *Elect* is one of the adjectives that can be used immediately after the noun only.
14 Wrong. *Sheer* is used attributively only.
15 Wrong. *Aghast* is used predicatively only.
16 Correct. Although *public* is not normally one of the adjectives that are used immediately after the noun, in connection with notary it is used in this way, as you will find when you look up *notary*. Therefore, in such cases

in which you cannot find the appropriate code in the adjective entry, it is always a good idea to try the noun entry before saying that a sentence is wrong. It may be right after all.

Abbreviations

1 aka = also known as
OTT = over the top
2 USN = United States Navy
GOP = Grand Old Party
MC = Member of Congress
3 RSPCA = Royal Society for the Prevention of Cruelty to Animals
NSPCC = National Society for the Prevention of Cruelty to Children
4 GCSE = General Certificate of Secondary Education
A Level = Advanced Level
NB = (Latin nota bene) take special notice
5 PM = Prime Minister
Rt Hon = Right Honourable
FCO = Foreign and Commonwealth Office
MEP = Member of the European Parliament
VIP = very important person
6 BA = Bachelor of Arts
MA = Master of Arts
QC = Queen's Counsel
7 CAD = computer-aided design
HQ = headquarters
WC = West Central

Labels

A
1 in jail – the others are all slang expressions for prison
2 polystyrene – the others are all proprietary names
3 buttocks – the others are all informal words for that part of the body
4 skinny – it is a derogatory word for thin, while the other words are approving
5 drivel – the others are all dated informal words for nonsense
6 saver – the others are all derogatory words for someone who is very careful with money
7 bonnet – it is British English, the others are all US words for parts of a car
8 latrine – the other words are euphemisms
9 council – the others are all legal terms

B
You would not be pleased to be described as *hoity-toity, namby-pamby, a clever Dick, birdbrained, straitlaced* or *grandiloquent* as all these words are derogatory when applied to a person, but *statuesque, masterly, a stalwart* and *a polymath* are all approving, so you would regard them as a compliment.

British, American and other varieties of English

A

1 James waited one floor higher up in the building than Bill because James uses British English and enters a building at ground floor level, whereas Bill, using American English, would say that when he enters the building he finds himself on the first floor. Consequently, Bill's second floor is only James's first floor. Cf. the note on usage at *floor*.

2 In America, the *subway* is an underground railway for which you need a ticket. In Britain, one would use the words *underground* or *tube* for such a train, whereas a *subway* in Britain is a tunnel under the road or railway through which people can walk. Of course, you don't need a ticket for it.

3 elevator.

4 *Suspenders*, in American English, are simply *braces* as they are usually worn by men to hold their trousers up, whereas in British English, *suspenders* are part of a woman's underwear. On the other hand, in American English, *garter* is another word for the British *suspender*. The *Order of the Garter*, as you can learn from the example at order[1] 11(a), is an ancient order of chivalry. It is a very high honour to be made a Knight of the Garter.

5 *Chips* in America are not a hot dish, but what the British call *crisps*. The American term for the British *chips* is *French fries*.

6 toilet.

7 The Fall refers to the scene in the Bible when Adam and Eve did not obey God and had to leave the Garden of Eden (cf. fall[2] 6). When Joey refers to *the fall*, he uses the American word for *autumn* (cf. fall[2] 5).

8 dual carriageways.

9 In Britain, you can be d*runk as a lord*, whereas in America you can be *drunk as a skunk*.

10 druggist's.

B

1 *Bug* is American English. So the speaker presumably comes from America.

2 *Step on the gas* is American English.

3 *Petrol station* is British English.

4 *Laird* is a Scottish word for landowner.

5 *Veld* is a South African word.

6 *Knock sb up* here is used in sense 1 and therefore is British (informal) English.

7 *Freight train* is American English.

8 *Jumble sale* is British English.

9 *Crook* is Australian (informal) English.

10 *Railroad* is American English.

11 *Station* in sense 5 is Australian English.

12 *Guy* in sense 1 (b) and *that's the way the cookie crumbles* are American English.

13 *Drawing-pins* is British English.

14 *Kook* is American English. It is derogatory slang.

15 *Different to* is British English.

C

theater, neighbors, realize (cf. the note on usage at -ize, ise), suspenders, automobile, hood, expressway/freeway/thruway, fall, sidewalk, tuxedo, quarreling, prolog, elevator, second, program, center, marvelous.

Prepositions

1 deaf to	6 scared of
2 jealous of	7 sensitive to
3 dependent on	8 greedy for
4 open to/full of	9 capable of
5 accustomed to	10 happy about

Cross-references

1 *giggle*, e.g.: The children couldn't stop giggling at the clown's funny songs.
titter, e.g.: The girls nervously tittered and chattered at the edge of the dance-floor.
(From the entry for *snigger*, follow the cross-reference to the note on usage at *giggle*).

2 If you follow the cross-reference from the entry at *deer-stalker* to the picture at *hat*, you will find that Sherlock Holmes could also have worn a *beret*, a *bowler* (which in America would have been called a *derby*), a *cap* (with *badge* and *peak*), a *top hat*, a *baseball cap*, a *stetson* (with a *wide brim*), a *flat cap*, a *fez*, a *skullcap* or a *woolly hat*.

3 Follow the cross-reference from the entry for *ton* to Appendix 2, and on p. 1336 you will find that a ton is a non-metric measure and has about 1016.04 kilograms, whereas a tonne is a metric measure and has exactly 1000 kilograms. We distinguish between metric and non-metric measures. The measures of weight in the metric system are milligrams, grams, and kilograms, whereas in the non-metric system they are grains, ounces, pounds, stone and hundredweight.

4 In the idioms section of the entry for the noun *time*, you can find the idiom *have a whale of a time*. If you then follow the cross-reference to *whale* and consult the idioms section there, you will find that *have a whale of a time* is an informal expression and means 'to enjoy one-self very much; to have a very good time,' such as in the sentence: *The children had a whale of a time at the fair.*

5 *ask, request, beg, entreat, implore, beseech* (Follow the cross-reference at *request* to the note on usage at *ask* in order to find these verbs).

6 Follow the cross-reference at *bungalow* to the picture at *house* and you will find: *row of terraced houses/terrace* (US *row houses*), *semi-detached houses* (US *duplex*), detached house (US *house*) and (on the following page) *bungalow* (US *ranch house*).

7 The different parts of the *leg* are: the *shin*, the *calf*, the *knee* and the *thigh* (Follow the cross-reference from the entry for *leg* to the picture at *human*).

8 *nudge, jab, poke, stab* (Follow the cross-reference from *prod* to the note on usage at *nudge*. There you find the four words with examples and an explanation of the differences between them).

9 Follow the cross-reference from *chrysalis* to the picture at *butterfly* and you will find that the chrysalis develops out of a caterpillar.

10 *Transepts* can be found in churches. Follow the cross-reference from *transept* to the picture at *church*, where you can find out that a church also can have a *porch*, *aisles*, a *nave*, *chapels*, a *choir*, a *chancel*, a *belfry* and a *vestry*. In the picture you will also find many more architectural terms and the names of the objects a church is furnished with.

11 *fog, mist, smog* (Follow the cross-reference from *haze* to the note on usage at *fog*. There you find the three words and an explanation of the difference between them).

12 *roasting pan, grill pan* (US *broiler pan*), *wok, frying-pan* (US *fry-pan*), *pressure cooker, saucepan* (Follow the cross-reference from *casserole* to the picture at *pan*).

13 *beautiful, pretty, good-looking, handsome, attractive*. Follow the cross-reference from *attractive* to the note on usage for *beautiful*. There you can find the five adjectives as well as an explanation of the differences between them. For examples look at the entries for the individual adjectives.

14 *chin-rest, bridge* and *strings* are three parts of a viola. The equivalent to a piccolo's mouthpiece in an oboe is called *reed* (to find this information, follow the cross-reference from *viola* to the picture at *musical instruments*).

15 *briefcase, suitcase, trunk* (Follow the cross-reference from *rucksack* to the picture at *luggage*).

16 If you consult the entry for *ago*, you will find a cross-reference to the note on usage at *recent*. There you find *not long ago, recently* and *lately* as well as examples and an explanation of the different usage of these words.

Usage notes

A

1 occasion	5 occasion
2 opportunity/chance	6 opportunities
3 possibility/chance	7 chance/opportunity
4 chances	8 possibilities

B

1 screamed	4 screamed/cried
2 shout	5 screaming/crying
3 yelled/shouted	6 screamed

C

1 a it's not allowed
  b it's not necessary or compulsory – don't eat it if you don't want to
  c as b
2 a your own decision
  b someone else has told you to
  c future – it is going to be necessary
3 a asking permission – is it allowed?
  b is it compulsory – have I no choice?
  c asking permission, or asking if it is physically possible
4 a logical deduction
  b perhaps she is – it is possible
  c as b

Idioms

A

1 cost an arm and a leg
2 you were pulling my leg
3 he talks the hind leg off a donkey
4 is on its last legs
5 with his tail between his legs
6 it's no skin off my nose
7 look down her nose at me
8 sticking/poking her nose into
9 follow your nose
10 gets up my nose

B

1 She looks as pretty as a picture.
2 He's as drunk as a lord.
3 He's as strong as an ox (or a horse).
4 He's as tough as old boots.
5 She's as bright as a button.
6 He's as miserable as sin.
7 It's as flat as a pancake.
8 She's as bold as brass.
9 It's as dry as a bone.
10 She's as nutty as a fruitcake.

Appendices

A

1 stride (Appendix 1, p. 1331).
2 dive, dwell, get, kneel, plead, quit, saw, spit (Appendix 1).
3 The asterisk (*) signifies that the alternative form *abode* can only be used in certain senses of the word *abide*, namely only in the archaic or formal use of the word with the meaning of *remain or stay in a place*, not when the meaning of *abide* is *tolerate or bear sb/sth*, as you will find if you consult the entry for abide.
4 *cleave* 'to split sth by chopping it with sth sharp and heavy', 'to make a way (through sth) esp by splitting it'; *pt:* cleaved, clove, cleft; *pp:* cleaved, cloven, cleft.

5 *Five hundred and sixty-seven* is correct both in British and in American English, *five hundred sixty-seven* can only be used in American English, as you can read in the section entitled 'Numbers over 100' in Appendix 2 (p. 1332).

6 *Half ten* means *half past ten*, but is only correct in an informal context (cf. Appendix 2, Telling the time, p. 1333).

7 The dentist comes from America, because *a quarter of ten* is American English. The patient says *ten thirty*, which is British English, so that s/he presumably comes from the British Isles (cf. Appendix 2, Telling the time, p. 1333).

8 ˌtwo ˌhundred and ˌforty-'nine (cf. Appendix 2 , Numbers over 100).

9 68/375 = sixty-eight over three seven five (cf. Appendix 2, Fractions).

10 B is inappropriate. We can say either 11 am or eleven o'clock in the morning, but we cannot combine the two (cf. Appendix 2, Telling the time, p. 1334).

11 'I hope it's OK if I open the window,' said the student in the first-class compartment. – 'Certainly not, young man', the elderly lady replied, 'because it would not be good for my asthma.' – The student retorted, 'If you've got asthma, why do you smoke?' (cf. Appendix 3, Quoting conversation).

12 My home town, which is surrounded by beautiful mountains, was snowed in last night. People who drink and drive should be sent to prison. (cf. Appendix 3, Comma. In the first sentence, the information offered between commas is additional, whereas in the second sentence the information offered in the relative clause is essential and therefore cannot be separated by commas from the rest of the sentence.)

B
Cousins, brother-in-law, Richard, Elizabeth, father-in-law, great grandmother, great granddaughter, sister-in-law (Appendices 4 and 5).

Word-division

The word processor made mistakes in the following cases (The hyphens indicate where the words could be divided instead): whether (cannot be divided), multi-fari-ous, mys-teri-ous, in-ter-pret-ed (see in-ter-pret-ation and in-ter-pret-er), ma-jor-ity, over-whelm-ing-ly, re-spon-sible, event (cannot be divided), after (cannot be divided), grand-mother.

Phrasal verbs
A

1 up	6 down
2 out	7 at
3 up	8 over
4 for	9 up
5 off	10 around

B

1 catch on	6 putting me off
2 done up	7 put you through to
3 fall back on	white wine
4 stands for	8 dropped off
5 keeps himself	9 drop in
to himself	10 pick you up
	11 pick on

Collocations

The point of the joke depends on a collocation. *Thin* is used of hair, and *fat* can be the opposite of *thin*, but *fat* is never used of hair. (Note that *fat* is not the equivalent of the German 'fett'.) Under *fat 3* in the dictionary you will find the synonym *thick*, and if you look up *thick 2* you will find the example 'His hair is thick and wavy', so *thick* would be the correct collocation, and to an English person the idea of *fat* hair is funny.

1 raw
2 chubby
3 candid
4 strict
5 bunch
6 beat, fold
7 mistakes, made

Word patterns and structures
A

1 Correct. Cf. *Would it help you to know that …?/This charity aims to help people to help themselves/I helped him to find his clothes.*

2 Correct. Cf. *This charity aims to help people help themselves/I helped him find his clothes.*

3 Correct. Cf. 1.

4 Wrong. No *-ing*-construction after *help*.

5 Correct. Cf. *He's been helping himself to my stationery.*

6 Wrong. No *that*-clause after *help*.

7 Correct. Cf. *He will be considered a weak leader.*

8 Correct. Cf. *consider sb as a candidate.*

9 Wrong. You can consider sb for a job, but only as a candidate.

10 Correct. Cf. 9.

11 Correct. Cf. We consider that you are not to blame.

12 Correct. Cf. *My boss doesn't allow me to use the telephone for private calls/Passengers are not allowed to smoke/Allow the water to come to boil/I didn't really want to go, but I allowed myself to be persuaded/She allowed her mind to wander.*

13 Correct. Cf. *You must allow three metres for a long-sleeved dress.*

14 Correct. Cf. *Photography is not allowed in the theatre/ We don't allow smoking in our house/The invention of printing allowed a huge increase in literacy.*

15 Correct. Cf. *He allowed that I had the right to appeal/ Even if we allow that the poet was mad ...*
16 Wrong. No infinitive-construction without *to* after *allow*.
17 Correct. Cf. *How much holiday are you allowed?/I'm not allowed visitors/I allow myself one glass of wine a day/He allowed his imagination free rein.*

B

1 from	6 for
2 to	7 on
3 in	8 up
4 down on	9 on
5 up to	10 forth, on

C

1 decide: [V.wh], e.g. *With so much choice, it's hard to decide what to buy/This last game will decide who is to be champion.*
[Vadv], e.g. *I wanted to be a painter, but circumstances decided otherwise.*
2 prevent: [V.n ing], e.g. *Nobody can prevent us getting married.*
[Vn], e.g. *Your prompt action prevented a serious accident/prevent the spread of a disease.*
3 raise: [Vnpr], e.g. *He raised his eyes from his work/raise a sunken ship (up) to the surface/He raised himself (up) on one elbow.*
4 start: [Vp], e.g. *We plan to start out at 6 o'clock/He started up from his seat.*
[V.ing], e.g. *He started laughing.*
5 remember: [V.wh], e.g. *Do you remember where you put the key?*
[V.n ing], e.g. *I remember him objecting to the scheme.*
6 invite: [Vn.to inf], e.g. *They invited me to come to their party/I've been invited to give a talk at the conference/ Leaving your car unlocked is just inviting someone to steal it.*
[Vnp], e.g. *invite sb round/in/up/He liked the girl and decided to invite her out.*
[Vnpr], e.g. *invite sb to/for dinner/Candidates will be invited for interview early next month/After his speech he invited questions from the audience.*
7 limit: None of the codes listed in the exercise fits the verb limit.
8 abide: [Vn], e.g. *I can't abide that man/How could you abide such awful conditions?*
[Vpr], e.g. *abide with sb/the right to enter and abide in a country.*
9 fail: [V.to inf], e.g. *The letter failed to arrive in time/He never fails to write to his mother every week/She failed to keep her appointment.*
[V], e.g. *The power failed as soon as I switched on the machine/The crops have failed again/Her eyesight is failing/His last months in office were marked by failing health/The brakes failed on the hill, but I managed to stop the car/Several banks failed during the recession.*
[Vpr], e.g. *I seem to fail in everything I do.*
[Vn], e.g. *He failed his driving test/The examiners failed*
over half the candidates/He felt he had failed his family by being unemployed/She promised that she wouldn't fail him/My courage failed me at the last minute.*
10 mix: [Vnn], e.g. *He mixed her a gin and tonic.*
[Vnp], e.g. *mix all the ingredients together.*

D

1 [Vn.wh], as in *Tell me where you live/This gauge tells you how much petrol you have left.*
2 [Vpr], as in *She has wisely refrained from criticizing the government in public.*
3 [V-adj], as in *look healthy/ill/pale/puzzled/sad/tired/That book looks interesting.*
4 [V.that], as in *I insist that you take immediate action to put this right/She kept insisting that she was innocent.*
5 [Vn.inf(no to)], as in *I saw you put the key in your pocket.*
6 [V.speech], as in *'Why is that?' Jill interrupted.*
7 [Vpr], as in *live to a great age/The doctors don't think he will live through the night/live at home/in London/in an apartment/The memory will live in my heart for ever.*
8 [Vnpr], as in *Stop throwing stones at the dog!/She threw it to me/The boat was thrown onto the rocks/She threw herself into his arms/I ran up and threw my arms round him/The party threw its weight behind the proposal/He threw a blanket over the injured man/The wrestler succeeded in throwing his opponent to the floor/Hundreds were thrown out of work/We were thrown into confusion by the news/The problem was suddenly thrown into sharp focus/throw doubt on the verdict/throw the blame on sb/throw threats/insults/accusations at sb/The trees threw long shadows across the lawn/She threw her voice to the crowd of onlookers.*
9 [V.ing], as in *Children love playing.*
10 [Vn.to inf], as in *We ordered him to leave immediately.*

Practice text: „The Stowaway"
1 The *Ark of the Covenant* is a large wooden box or cupboard in which the writings of Jewish law were originally kept.
2 Sense 2(b): *a section of a stable or cattle shed for one animal.*
3 *tails.*
4 *Cheetahs* are African wild animals of the cat family with black spots and long legs. They would certainly have eaten the antelopes if they had been put within a short distance of them. The pronunciation of *antelope* is /ˈæntɪləʊp/.
5 *impossible to avoid, unavoidable.*
6 *curfew, isolation cells, stool pigeons, ratting, prison ship.*
7 *stool pigeons, ratting, of ours, rock the boat.*
8 The narrator certainly does not mean he has a banking problem. He does not use *account* in senses 1 to 3, but in sense 4, 'a report or description of an event'.

9 The much repeated *version* is the *Bible*. *Version* here is used in sense 1. Therefore, *account* would be a good synonym.

10 *fascinates, pleases, attracts, delights.*

11 /'skeptɪk/. The British spelling *sceptic* is no help because other words with sc-, such as *scenery*, are only pronounced with a /s/ at the beginning. The American spelling, *skeptic*, however, can indeed be a good help in remembering the pronunciation.

12 A *compendium* is a collection of detailed items, here the animals' sentimental myths, esp in a book. *Compendium* has two plural forms, *compendiums* and *compendia*.

13 *Myth* is a particularly appropriate word here because a myth often is a story concerning the early history of a people or explaining natural events, such as the seasons. In our text, the myths explain the early history of the animals and the Flood.

14 No, he isn't. *Rock the boat* is an idiom in English and it means *to do sth that upsets a delicate situation and causes difficulties*. Here he means that the animals will not publicly doubt the official version of the Flood as it is told in the Bible.

15 The animals have been *considered as* heroes/*described as* heroes in the Biblical account of the Flood and in their own sentimental myths (treat 2).

16 The infinitive of *chosen* is *choose*. The spelling can be a problem because of the question of whether there is one *o* or two. In the verb *lose*, for example, the infinitive has only one *o*. The word *loose* with double *o*, on the other hand, is an adjective with a different meaning. Words with similar meanings to that of *choose* are *select, pick* and *opt for*. You can find them and the differences between them in the note on usage at *choose*.

17 The phenomenon described here is that of *collocation*.

18 The opposite of *convenient* is *inconvenient*. The animals' lapses of memory are convenient because they help them and others forget the negative aspects of the voyage on board the ark as well as of their early history.

19 Another word for *constrained* here might be *restricted*. The corresponding noun is *constraint*.

20 A *stowaway* is 'a person who hides in a ship or an aircraft before its departure, in order to travel without paying or being seen'. The word probably came into existence because it describes someone who *stows himself away*, i.e. hides himself.

21 *prospered.*

22 The stowaway considers himself a little *set apart* from the others, i.e. *different from them*. He is proud of this because the term implies that he is superior to the others.

23 Sense 2: 'a social gathering of people who were formerly friends'.

24 The term *sea legs* describes 'the ability to walk easily on the deck of a moving ship and not to feel sick at sea', an ability that was certainly very useful on board the ark.

25 The narrator uses the word *voyage* because on board the ark, he made a long journey by sea. The activity of travelling can be described with the help of the words *jour-ney, voyage, travels, tour, trip* and *excursion*. You can find the differences between these words in the note on usage at the entry for *journey*. The narrator spells *Voyage* with a capital V because to him, the time on the ark was the *Voyage* of his life, i.e. the most extraordinary undertaking he will ever experience. It saved his life, made him a survivor, and enabled him to tell us his story.

26 A *sense of obligation* usually comes from one's *conscience* (cf. obligation b).

27 gratitude *to* sb *for* sth

28 /smɪə(r)/ and /'væsəliːn/.

29 The narrator means that, since he does not idealize the voyage on the ark and has nothing to be grateful for, he wants to remain objective and give a truthful account of what happened rather than provide us with a version that looks at the ark through rose-tinted spectacles. The narrator claims that his account is the correct one.

30 Despite his claim to truthfulness, the narrator is not an objective reporter. He had to spend his time on the ark as a stowaway and would not have been accepted on board if he had officially asked for admittance. As a woodworm, he ranks low in the hierarchy of the animal kingdom and receives little respect from the others. Moreover, although he says that we can trust his account, he does not always use neutral language, such as when he describes the ark as a military dictatorship or when he uses informal language in order to make the reader feel closer to him. Consequently, even though the narrator may give us an interesting new version of what happened on board the ark, it need not necessarily be a disinterested version, and we should not trust him blindly.

Pre-eminent scientists

A

1 civic 1 – of a town or city. MUNICIPAL is a cross-reference to a word with similar meaning.

2 The adjective is normally *banqueting*.

3 A *contestant* is any person who is taking part in a contest, a *finalist* is someone who has reached the final stage of a contest or competition.

4 No. Under *music* you find the compound *music-hall* defined as 'a theatre where shows with a variety of entertainments were presented'.

5 A *final* is the last of a series of contests, or the last of a set of university exams. A *finale* is the last part of a piece of music or a drama.

6 EU = European Union

7 No. Here it means 'an instance of sth occurring'.

8 fair 3 – *an exhibition of commercial and industrial goods.* If you follow the cross-reference to the note at *exhibition* you find the words *show, display* and *demonstration.*

9 *encourage, promote. Foster parents.*

10 It means Europe has plenty of scientific talent, the expression is ironic, or understated. hardly 5; short 3a.

11 Yes, he describes it as *ingenious*, which means *original and well-suited to its purpose*.

12 Other examples given in the entry for *retract* are to *retract a confession, a promise* or *an offer*.

13 in mathematics (cf. label before the definition).

14 a person, clothes, tastes (cf. examples under *sophisticated*).

15 He (or she) is young, not yet a qualified biologist, but with the ambition or desire to be one.

16 3. The team is a trio.

17 Shade 6 – *degree or depth of colour. Shades* can mean *sunglasses*.

18 to make sth dirty.

19 sap. It can also mean a stupid person.

20 To *wilt* can be used of people, in the sense of growing weak or tired, eg spectators wilting in the heat.

21 envision

22 a top, a sewing machine, a moth's wings.

23 away 2 – continuously. The machine kept on whirring, making a steady, low noise.

24 The definition given under *loopy* is crazy, which doesn't make sense here. If you look at the word *loop* above, you find a definition that fits better, and an example referring to handwriting.

25 The *British Association's Festival of Science* and the *EU Contest for Young Scientists* are different in size and scope. The EU contest is a much smaller event (*dwarfed* by the British Association). They are alike in that there are very few female scientists involved.

B

1	contestants	6	wilt
2	short	7	ingenious
3	civic	8	soil
4	foster, counterparts	9	shade
5	sophisticated	10	cases

Bilgewater

A

1 17

2 Yorkshire, England

3 Marigold Daisy Green

4 Bilgewater

5 No ('it seems a great bitterness')

6 Her father's name is Bill, *Bill's daughter* rhymes with and sounds a bit like *Bilgewater*.

B

1 *Old-fashioned* means *out of date. Fashioned-old* comes from the verb *to fashion*, meaning *to give form or shape to sth*, or *to design or make sth*, and *old* in sense 2 – *no longer young*. Marigold thinks that her character and appearance are not those of a child, but of an old person, she is not quite in keeping with the times or with her own age.

2 The first time *emerge* is used in the first sense given in the dictionary – *to come out of a place*, here as a synonym for *being born*. The second time it could simply be a repetition of the first use, but it could also have something to do with the second meaning (2a) – d*eveloping and becoming noticeable*, as she describes her development from baby to adolescent.

3 for[1] 5 – indicating reason or cause, *because of, on account of*.

4 *short-sighted* and *slithery-pupilled*.

5 *frog-bodied* means *having the body or shape of a frog*. Other examples given are *big-bodied, able-bodied* and *full-bodied*.

6 pupil[2] – *dark circular opening in the centre of the eye*. The other meaning is *a child who is taught*.

7 No. You have to look at the first entry for the verb *blink* – *to shut and open the eyes quickly*.

8 hanging about and idle

9 No. *Housemaster* means *a male teacher in charge of a school house* – and *master of the house* refers to *the male head of a private household*.

10 *Broomsticks* are associated with witches. The boys were implying that Marigold looked like a witch.

11 She had orange hair, the colour of the marigold, an orange flower.

12 If you look up the word *bilgewater*, you will find that it means *the dirty water that collects in the bottom of a ship*, and also, in slang, *worthless talk or nonsense*. In both senses it is something unpleasant, that nobody could admire or respect. Marigold thinks very little of herself and believes that no one finds her attractive, so the name seems suitable.

13 No, the last syllable of the verb is pronounced differently /ə'prəʊprɪeɪt/.

C

1	hilarity	5	quaint
2	solemn	6	slithery
3	for	7	appropriate
4	cloisters	8	idle